Greater Than Fear

Defeating a Cultural Pandemic

By Jeremy Gove

"Of all the liars in the world, sometimes the worst are our own fears."
~Rudyard Kipling

This book is published by:

FoxFire Media
935 Azalea Street
Blackshear, GA 31516
www.foxfiremedia.org

The cover art and all graphics have been created by the same.

Every effort has been made to identify and trace copyright holders and to obtain their permission for the use of copyrighted material. The publisher apologizes for any errors or omissions and would be grateful if notified of any corrections that should be incorporated in future reprints or editions of this book.

All Scripture references are taken from the King James Version, unless otherwise noted. Other versions of the Bible referenced in this work include:

NIV
THE HOLY BIBLE, NEW INTERNATIONAL VERSION®, NIV® Copyright © 1973, 1978, 1984, 2011 by Biblica, Inc.® Used by permission. All rights reserved worldwide.

Table of Contents

Before We Begin

This booklet was written with a specific purpose: **to disarm the dynasty of doubt.** With the threat of a global pandemic and economic crisis, politicians and pundits alike are ever feeding into the frenzy of fear. This is not how life was meant to be. Instead, one of the most powerful benefits of living for Jesus Christ is the provision of hope.

I remember a particular instance while I was in college. I was juggling a full-time schedule, management of a small business, and working as a first-time Youth Pastor (this was long before the term "Student Pastor" came into vogue). That specific semester had been especially grueling. Hard classes, long hours, and the knowledge in the back of my mind that no matter what I did, I still had to work when I got home. I remember I was also struggling with how to handle a rough student who was causing problems in our youth group. I guess you could say she was more street than saved. I chuckle a bit when I think of that today, but struggles are relative, and I was new, inexperienced, and overwhelmed.

I had just finished my classes for the day and was headed to the bus stop. From there I would catch my ride to off-campus parking where I would pick up my car and start on my 40-minute commute home. The entire time, I felt I was under mental attack: *"You're not good enough. Who do you think you are? You don't have what it takes."* Those kinds of thoughts began to snowball.

Even though it made no sense (my classes were hard, but I was doing well), I began to wonder if I would pass my classes. Then that progressed to a worry about whether I would graduate on time. Then, I began to think about my teens and question if I was really doing them any good with the work I was doing. Then, I began to think about my family business. What if it failed? It was the only thing paying my tuition bill. On and on it went, spiraling out of control. A dark cloud suddenly came out of nowhere and completely enveloped my life. Fear was everywhere.

Utterly overwhelmed, I finally made it to my car. I cranked it up and just sat. A modern worship chorus drifted softly through the radio and gently filled my car with praise. It was there in that moment that I did the only thing I knew to do. I prayed.

It wasn't some earth-shattering prayer either. We're talking two-to-three sentences at most, with a lot of *"what do I do's?"* sprinkled between. I shifted my car into "drive" and pulled out of the University of Delaware Field House parking lot onto 896. Shortly after, I crossed the boundary-line of campus and, suddenly, it was like someone flipped a light switch. I immediately felt relieved.

The Spirit of the Lord quickened me and said, *"You've never known what it's like to be without My Presence. You've always known My Peace. But I've allowed you to experience the absence of hope, so you can know how life feels for those who don't know Me."* Needless to say, I had to pull over, to weep and to worship.

While that was a monumental moment for me and helped establish compassion in my heart, it also did something else. It caused me to cherish the peace and hope that comes with knowing Jesus Christ. Today, years later, I don't take that hope for granted. The peace, love, hope, faith, and power of God is greater than fear can ever dream to be. I pray you are encouraged by the words in this book. I pray they propel you into a deeper level of faith.

No matter what anyone else says. Remember, God is greater than fear.

Sincerely,

Jeremy Gove
Student Pastor, Truth Tabernacle - Blackshear, GA
www.foxfiremedia.org | www.jeremygove.com

CHAPTER ONE

Doubt is Not Your Friend

"Have not I commanded thee? Be strong and of a good courage; be not afraid, neither be thou dismayed: for the Lord thy God is with thee whithersoever thou goest."
(Joshua 1:9)

As Joshua stood on the banks of the Jordan River, I imagine the landscape before him appeared to double in size. It's only natural to perceive the terrain rather than the triumph. After all, he was a human being of flesh, blood, and emotions like the rest of us. With God's command still ringing fresh in his ears, he turned to the people and relayed the message: *"In three days, we cross and conquer."* (Joshua 1:9)

Joshua's mentor, Moses, had recently passed away and this was his first major undertaking as Israel's new leader. As such, it would be more than a standard conquest. The success or failure of this endeavor would potentially set the pace for the remainder of his leadership tenure.

Would he be good enough? Strong enough? Smart enough? Would he have what it would take to accomplish the task before him? Would he have a true chance, not just to survive and maintain, but to thrive and conquer? Joshua was in uncharted territory, literally and figuratively. He was on the cusp of leading an inexperienced generation into an unknown land. He had been there, of course. A leader can only lead where he's gone before. Years prior, he had bravely snuck into the Promised Land under the cover of night as a spy. But there's a difference between reconnaissance and combat. And this time, he wouldn't be alone. It was his responsibility as Israel's Commander-in-Chief to lead a fledgling multitude of aimless wanderers and transform them into formidable soldiers, masters of war.

Understanding the weight of the matter, it's no wonder God phrased His command to Joshua the way He did. Two times within a span of three verses, the same statement is made. But it's more than a charge for action; it's a command coupled with a promise.

Since He is the All-Knowing One, I can't help but believe God purposefully tailored His words to fit Joshua's unique circumstances. God always speaks with purpose. He minces no words. In a handful of statements, He addresses every misgiving and potential pitfall Israel's new leader might have. It's to this specific set of circumstances God Almighty proclaims the following:

"Only be thou strong and very courageous, that thou mayest observe to do according to all the law, which Moses my servant commanded thee: turn not from it to the right hand or to the left, that thou mayest prosper withersoever thou goest." (Joshua 1:7)

"Have not I commanded thee? Be strong and of a good courage; be not afraid, neither be thou dismayed: for the Lord thy God is with thee whithersoever thou goest." (Joshua 1:9)

There's an operative word in both of these verses. I'm sure you're thinking I'm going to say *"strong"* or *"courageous."* Those are the words we cling to the most. But the word I want to point out, is much more subtle and, I would argue, even more important than the others.

It's this word: **Be.**

Earth-shattering, right? It may not seem that way, but it is. Because God deals in realities. He doesn't tell Joshua to <u>feel</u> strong and courageous. He tells him to <u>be</u> strong and courageous. He doesn't tell him to never <u>feel</u> fear. He tells him not to <u>be</u> afraid. He doesn't tell

Joshua to never know what it <u>feels</u> like to be overwhelmed and dismayed. Instead, He tells him to refuse to <u>be</u> dismayed.

On one hand, we empathize with Joshua because he's given what seems like an impossible task. But that's where the promise comes into play. Because God doesn't just give Joshua a "what," He answers Joshua's "why."

Why are you strong? Because God is with you. Why can you have courage? Because God will protect you when you refuse to turn to the right or to the left. Why aren't you afraid? Because you have a Word directly from the Lord to move forward.

The circumstances are still the same, Joshua. The enemy is still the same. The territory is just as large and the task is just as daunting as it was before. But no matter how you feel, no matter what you see, and no matter what you hear, you can <u>be</u> strong and you can <u>be</u> courageous because your God is greater than your fear!

It's imperative to understand, acknowledging fear is not the same as being afraid. Knowing it exists doesn't provide it any power. There's a difference between knowing fear exists and letting fear have ownership. It's not wrong to feel a twinge of fear. It's not a bad thing to know what disappointment feels like. But, problems arise when we allow our feelings to take hold and form our reality.

That's why God phrases His challenge to Joshua as a command. At the end of the day, courage is a choice. Courage is when we say: *"I acknowledge fear exists, but I refuse to allow it to control me."* Still, we need not be reckless; we must use common sense and continue to pray, plan, and prepare. Because our primary focus is not on the untamed territory before us, but on the untapped triumph that has been promised to us. If God has said it, He will do it!

Victory may require the blood, sweat, and tears of sacrifice. The promise of success never comes without a price. Joshua may have had a

Word from God, but he still had a work to do for God. What I find to be the most beautiful part of this story is that God doesn't deal in empty promises. Instead, he equips Joshua to do what He has called him to do. Joshua's primary responsibility is the same one we have today: *Trust in the Lord.*

DOUBT IS NOT YOUR FRIEND

Contained this story is a subtle truth I believe God wants us to understand: **Doubt is not your friend.** It's tempting to view doubt as a ticket to authenticity. Sadly, doubt is quickly trending in modern-day Christian culture. Just recently, my social media feed exploded with posts from several friends sharing the "revelation" of a certain pastor who openly championed and encouraged the presence of doubt, calling it a gift from God. Most concerning is that it isn't an isolated incident. At a rate of what feels like at least once a month, I hear of another pastor stepping into their pulpit, onto their platform, or up on their stage, telling their congregations doubt is a virtue.

The idea is to foster authenticity. It's meant to remove barriers and create a sense of transparency. This same movement holds that our doubts make us stronger and embracing them will draw us closer to God. But the reality couldn't be further from the truth. Doubt is not the basic requirement to please God, *__faith__* is! (Hebrews 11:6)

Our authenticity should be expressed through faith. Authentic faith says, *"God, You are God and I am not. I don't understand all of the details, but I know You are in control."* When this happens, fear loses its influence. Authentic faith refuses to give fear a stronghold.

We can search the Scriptures exhaustively, but we will never find a verse commanding us to doubt. The more we read, the more we see the opposite — a call to trust. While there is no single instance of a command to doubt, it's fitting there are at least 365 commands to "fear not" and to "be not afraid" in Scripture—at least one for each day of the year.

The worst possible ingredient we can add to our lives is doubt. Fittingly so, Scripture tells us to do the opposite. In II Peter 1:5-7, the Apostle Peter writes: *"And beside this, giving all diligence, add to your faith virtue; and to virtue knowledge; And to knowledge temperance; and to temperance patience; and to patience godliness; And to godliness brotherly kindness; and to brotherly kindness charity."* (II Peter 1:5-7)

Notice, Peter challenges us to add to our faith, assuming that faith is already present. In the opening verse of the chapter, he calls it *"like precious faith"* (II Peter 1:1). The word "like" there is better translated as "similar" or "matching." Peter is rejoicing that the faith of this particular church is the same as his own.

Rejoicing in similar faith is a powerful concept. After all, the Scripture is of no private interpretation (II Peter 1:20). Faith is universal; doubt is individual.

Every atheist I've ever met shares a common narrative. They each have their own individual "losing faith" story. Each one has a unique problem, concept, or tragedy they point to and say, *"This is the moment I lost my faith. Right here, at this particular time, is when I stopped believing in God."* Doubt is individual.

Faith is universal. It has an individual component, too. It simply works in a different way. In order for faith to be **our** faith, we have to individually accept it, but here's the catch: **The principles of Faith are true whether we believe them or not.** I can doubt gravity all I want, but that doesn't change the outcome if I jump out my window. Doubt, on the other hand, is fully controlled by us. We can't understand and so we doubt. We don't see the reason and so we doubt. We don't like the outcome and so we doubt.

Let's get back to Peter and faith. The Apostle celebrates that the church's "like" faith is similar to his own. Then, Peter adds a second word to his description of faith. He calls it "precious." The word "precious" here means exactly what we think, and then some. It describes an item of exceedingly costly value. It is second to none, the best of the best. That alone should inform our mindset regarding faith and doubt. If faith is that highly regarded, then conversely, doubt is disregarded in equal measure. The more we embrace faith, the further we displace doubt. The more we revere one, the more we renounce the other.

Lastly, the faith Peter describes is more than a religious creed or a stale, stagnant statement of beliefs. Yes, we should know what we believe and be able to express it. But, faith by definition is dynamic. It ebbs and flows, saturating our lives. That's one reason why I love II Peter 1:4, the verse immediately preceding the command to add to our faith. The beginning of this verse puts it this way: *"Whereby are given unto us exceeding great and precious promises..."* (II Peter 1:4).

In other words, the faith we have is actionable. It doesn't stop at a statement of belief. Instead, faith flourishes into full-blown trust. It's a trust that says, like the old song proclaims:

If Jesus said it, I believe it
His Word cannot lie
If it's written in the Bible
I'll believe it till I die
Though the mountains be removed
And cast into the sea
God's Word will last forever
Throughout eternity! [1]

We don't doubt His promises; we rely upon them! No matter what the circumstances may say, we know the promises of God are *"exceeding great and precious!"* (II Peter 1:4) It's fitting that the writer of Hebrews encourages us to mix together our faith and the Word of God (Hebrews 4:2). After all, *"faith cometh by hearing and hearing by the Word of God"* (Romans 10:17). Again, you will never find a Biblical command to doubt.

---

1 Lacour, Mildred Sullivan. "Jesus Said It, I Believe It." © Sept 21, 1944; E pub. 126557; James P. Sullivan, Lincoln, Neb. 48678

No matter how it presents itself, doubt is not your friend. And, doubt finds its basis in fear. We should never seek to build our lives with fear as the foundation. Doubt is never kind. It destroys trust and upheaves relationships. The moment a seed of doubt is planted in a relationship, the relationship begins to wither and die.

I have yet to see a flourishing marriage where the secret to their success was adding doubt to the mix. Think about it. Is your marriage stronger if you doubt your partner? Is a friendship stronger if you doubt your friend's faithfulness? Is your workplace better if you doubt your employer's intentions or integrity? Doubt destroys relationships. And if all of that is true with earthly relationships, how much more does it apply to our relationship with God?

It's time to click the de-friend button on doubt.

MARY AND ZACHARIAS
In the opening chapter of Luke, we have two very similar, yet very different conversations with God. Both involve questions, both deal with the impossible, and for both, the problem revolves around biology and babies.

Both Zacharias and Mary are told they will have a son. We of course, know Zacharias will be the father of John the Baptist, the preparer of the way, and Mary will be the mother of Jesus, the Way Himself. Upon hearing the news, each one responds in turn with a question.

- In Luke 1:18, Zacharias asks: *"How shall I know this?"*
- In Luke 1:34, Mary asks: *"How shall this be?"*

If we breeze over this passage, like we usually do, it sounds like the same question, but it's not. Look closer. With the way Zacharias speaks, he addresses God and says: *"How can I know this will happen? How do I know I can trust You?"* Contrast that with Mary, who says: *"I believe You. I know this will happen. But how?"*

Similar words, but worlds apart. Mary's question is about God. Zachariah's question is about himself. One assumes God will do something great and is curious about the details. The other wants proof that God will come through. One response is based in faith; one is based in doubt.

Here's where the rubber meets the road: **When faced with the impossible, which question do we find ourselves asking?** It isn't a matter of whether or not we'll have questions. It's a matter of what kind of questions we will have.

WAVES OF THE SEA

In James 1:6, the Bible says: *"But let him ask in faith, nothing wavering. For he that wavereth is like a wave of the sea driven with the wind and tossed."*

It's interesting that the word "wavereth" there is best translated as "doubting." No matter what the trendy preachers may say, the Bible has nothing but negative things to say about doubt. But, catch the analogy here. James says that the person who doubts is as stable as water.

Water is one of the most unstable elements on earth. It's a liquid. It flows, drips, and collapses. Remove one element, it disappears. Remove another, it becomes explosive.

I've seen it first-hand. My Dad has always been a bit of an inventor. From fixing items around the house, to building guitars and harps from scratch, to turning intricate ink pens, constructing remote controlled lawn-mowers, and programing 3D printers, he's done it all. It seems like every time we talk, he's working on a new project. I love that about him. He never sits idle; his mind and hands are ever-working. I guess that's where I get it from. It's fitting then, that outside of pastoring a church in Delaware, he works in research and development for a large Fortune 500 during the week. But years prior to that, I was in college, living at home while I attended classes. Per usual, we arrived at the weekend and I was outside working with him on his latest project. This time, his goal was to create a hydrogen-powered engine for a car.

I'm not too keen on the specifics, but I remember the first step was to separate hydrogen from oxygen in water. It involved a long PVC pipe, some heat, and an electrical current. I was there mostly to be a second set of eyes and hands. We were extremely careful, keeping a proper distance and care. But, upon our first attempt, once the hydrogen separated from the oxygen, it immediately ignited and KAPOW! We had a small burst of fireworks.

I've never seen my Mom run faster in my entire life. She came busting through the front door! *"Are you alright?!"* she yelled. To which, without skipping a beat, eyes still locked on the controls, both of us gave a thumbs up in unison and said, *"We're ok!"*

Water is extremely unstable and dangerous in the wrong conditions. At the same time, water is a critical component of life. It's essential to our very existence. We can't live without water.

Just like we can't live without water, we will never be able to live life without a semblance of instability. The question isn't whether or not life will be unstable. Rather, the real concern is, will we be unstable with it?

When I read this passage, and begin to think about water, I tend to also think about Peter walking out on the sea to Jesus. I don't know if you've ever tried it, but successfully walking on water is a pretty big deal. I know Jesus must still be working on me because I haven't been able to do it. It's a miraculous event when Jesus walks on the water and then invites Peter to come join Him.

In an act of radical faith, Peter steps out on the most unstable element known to man. He stands on something that should collapse under his feet. Peter's no novice either. If anyone knew water, Peter did. He had grown up on it. He knew the danger. He knew, better than most, just how impossible it really was.

And, incredibly, as he begins walking, everything is fine. Instability has become stable, because his eyes are on Jesus. His faith is where it should be and His trust is intact.

Then something happens.

A wave catches his eye, thunder catches his ear, the wind catches his face, and the storm catches his attention. Just because Peter stepped out of the boat didn't mean the storm stopped raging. The invitation to experience the miraculous never happens when the sea is calm.

The storm catches his attention and as Peter turns his eyes, he sees the turmoil and the chaos. He takes in the unstable elements around him. He identifies with them and begins to focus on the storm.

And, just like James says, the foundation beneath his feet becomes unstable. Faith gives way to fear. Suddenly, the realization of just how impossible and crazy this whole situation really is, hits him. He begins to sink and cries out and *"immediately Jesus stretched forth His hand, and caught him, and said unto him, 'O thou of little faith, wherefore didst thou doubt?'"* (Matthew 14:31)

Can you hear the disappointment in His Voice? Can you feel the hurt? That's how Jesus feels about doubt. Jesus says, *"I'm here, Peter. Why did you doubt? Doubt is not your friend, I am."*

And just like it was with Peter, Jesus is here. He's holding out His Hand. No matter the wind, no matter the waves, no matter the chaos, no matter all of the unknowns we face in our society today, faith has the capacity to overthrow fear.

Doubt is not your friend. Your Friend is the One who sticketh closer than a brother (Proverbs 18:24). Your Friend is the One Who said: *"I'll never leave you, nor forsake you"* (Hebrews 13:5). Your friend is the

Savior in the storm, extending His Hand, inviting you to take part in the miraculous. Will you trust Him?

CHAPTER TWO

The Big Three

"For God hath not given us the spirit of fear;
but of power, and of love, and of a sound mind."
(II Timothy 1:7)

I blame the movie *Jaws*, or at least the clips I caught in passing as a kid. It wasn't much, but it did the trick.

From that moment on, I was terrified of sharks. I enjoyed swimming, but only for short periods of time. Bath time was fun, but could only last so long. When it came to the ocean, I would only wade out waist deep and then run back to shore. I was much more excited about the boardwalk than the billowing waves.

As a result of my fear, I had a pretty odd habit at home. Whenever I saw footage of a shark, or thought about the ocean, I would quickly jump onto our living room couch as if to get away. In my mind, the couch was a tall, hulking ship, big enough and strong enough to reduce my worry. It was a reaction that did absolutely nothing for me, but made me feel safe.

It's a cute story. All kids and parents have them. I often wonder if my little girl will try and do the same kinds of things one day. I've already seen on the ultrasounds that she squirms and wiggles, struggling to sit still, just like her daddy. But another part of me hopes she doesn't, because I don't want her to irrationally fear. I want to teach my little girl to be brave.

There are plenty of rational fears. And there are instances in Scripture where we're commanded to fear, especially to fear the Lord. The fear of the Lord is the beginning of knowledge (Proverbs 1:7) and wisdom (Proverbs 9:10). It is the prolonger of days (Proverbs 10:27) and a fountain of life (Proverbs 14:27). But that type of fear is better expressed as respect. Fear, as we tend to think of it, operates quite differently. It is based on feelings, while respect is based on reality.

If I were dead-dropped into the middle of the ocean, my fear of sharks would probably be justified. As one comedian said, If I go to ocean, then I'm going to the shark's house and I can expect to be on the menu. [2] But outside of that, the fear serves no purpose other than to plague my mind.

Many times, we react to fear the way I used to react to my fear of sharks. We end up acting rashly and doing things that make us feel better, but ultimately serve no purpose. We theorize about all the ways things could go wrong. We sit in our house and shake. We stay up late doing Google searches and reading posts on medical forums and Facebook. We read up on all the weird ways situations like ours have turned sideways for others. These empty actions are ineffective at best and damaging at worse. In Proverbs 28:1, Solomon addresses this tendency saying, *"The wicked flee when no man pursueth: but the righteous are bold as a lion."* Wicked or not, we've all been there, running from a nonexistent pursuer.

There's a difference between identifying fear and allowing fear to be the source of our identity. Am I saying we should be reckless? Am I saying we should never utilize common sense or caution? Not at all. But we also cannot make a habit of running from the wind. Fear is big enough as it is; we don't need to add to its stature or influence in our lives.

As I said before, there are very real fears. There are legitimate instances that require our very real respect and attention. Ironically,

[2] Nash-Poleate, Veronica-Pooh. "Stay Outta the Shark's House!!!"
https://www.youtube.com/watch?v=boV0t-riFuw. Posted July 7, 2015. Accessed April 27, 2020.

researchers have found 85% of what worries us never happens. But what about the remaining 15%? It's interesting that in the same study, 79% of the participants found when their worries came true, they brought about a positive result. They were either able to turn the situation around because they were prepared or they were able to learn a valuable life lesson from the experience. [3]

That's why Paul wrote in Philippians 4:6: *"Be careful for nothing; but in every thing by prayer and supplication with thanksgiving let your requests be made known unto God."* The word "careful" is better translated as "anxious." Be anxious for nothing. It's not bad to feel a twinge of nervousness regarding the unknown. It's not even wrong to have an anxious thought. The problem starts when we allow anxiety to consume us, making us anxious worry-warts, afraid to take any action.

THE BIG THREE

The Bible is clear, God is greater than our fear. And not only is He greater, but He's supplied us with tools that are also greater than fear. We can't talk about the Bible and fear and not mention what I call "The Big Three." These are three elements God has promised and provided His people to overcome fear, uncertainty, and discouragement. All three are contained in II Timothy 1:7, *"For God hath not given us the spirit of fear; but of power, and of love, and of a sound mind."*

Before we get into the Big Three, I want you to notice the beginning of that verse. God has not given us the spirit of fear. God Himself has told us not to be afraid. But what about sickness? What about my job? What about the economy? What about my kids? What about my house? On and on we go with our list because there's no limit to the number of situations that tempt us to fear.

Paul's words to Timothy could not have come at a better time. He isn't spouting empty platitudes or postulating theological theorems in a

---

[3] Borkovec, Thomas & Hazlett-Stevens, Holly & Diaz, M.L. "The Role of Positive Beliefs about Worry in Generalized Anxiety Disorder and its Treatment." Clinical Psychology & Psychotherapy. 1999. 6. Page 129.

vacuum. Timothy, Paul's protégé and son in the faith, is in trouble. He's no doubt written Paul explaining the dire circumstances of his church and this epistle is Paul's response back. Timothy is the young pastor of the church in Ephesus, the largest church in the ancient world. At the writing of I Timothy, the church is gaining momentum and is on the rise, but by II Timothy the political landscape has radically changed.

Nero is now Emperor of the Roman Empire. Public opinion has become violently opposed to Christianity. Prior to this, the Early Church had been mostly persecuted by the Jews. But now, even the government has stepped in and started killing Christians. At this time in history, the church in Ephesus doesn't seem to be growing anymore. As more and more Christians are sought out, hunted, imprisoned, enslaved, and killed, there's a shift in the membership. Large groups of people begin to leave the church, reject Christianity, and go back to their old pagan temples—because it's just easier.

The real enemy of the church here isn't Nero. It's fear. Fear has a death-grip on Timothy's pastorate. It's to this environment, seven verses in, before Paul has even started to gain momentum, that he pens and proclaims: *"For God hath not given us the spirit of fear; but of power, and of love, and of a sound mind." (II Timothy 1:7)*

I imagine Paul motioning to himself as he writes, rocking, swaying, almost shouting: *"No matter what it looks like, Timothy! No matter what the world may do! No matter what society may say! No matter how loud the skeptics scream and the scoffers scorn! FEAR NOT! Nero may rule the known world. But he is not the One on the Ultimate Throne! God is greater than your fear!"*

And God in his greatness and goodness has given us tools for success against fear. The pandemic of fear has a cure. It is faith in the One True God. This faith is expressed when we utilize the tools He has given and expect them to work. They are **power**, **love**, and a **sound mind.**

POWER

God has not given us the spirit of fear, but He has given us another Spirit—the Holy Spirit. The word for "power" in II Timothy 1:7 is *dunamis*. It's the same word used to describe the power of the Holy Ghost in Acts 1:8: *"But ye shall receive **power**, after that the Holy Ghost is come upon you: and ye shall be witnesses unto Me both in Jerusalem, and in all Judaea, and in Samaria, and unto the uttermost part of the earth."*

The power described by the word *dunamis* is beyond "powerful." *Dunamis* is the root word of what we commonly call "dynamite." It's the explosive, dynamic, Earth-shattering, foundation-shaking, barrier-breaking Power of God!

Dynamite as we know it, is more commonly called TNT. In the natural, TNT stands for trinitrotoluene. It's the standard measure of all bombs and explosives. Every other explosive material and every other explosion itself is measured using TNT as a baseline. Just as the performance of a car motor is measured in horsepower, you could say explosives are measured in TNT-power.

When Jesus says His followers have *dunamis*, it means that through the Holy Ghost, they have everything they need to get the job done! No matter what skills they brought to the table. No matter what they could or couldn't do. No matter what society thought or said. No matter how unqualified they were going into the Upper Room. When they emerged on the Day of Pentecost, they were qualified to be witnesses, to do miracles, to make disciples, to walk in purpose, to walk in power, and to walk in authority. They were qualified to be overcomers. They were qualified to be victorious.

Why? Because they had *dunamis*. They had TNT. They had everything they needed, regardless of talent. Don't sell yourself short! The most explosive, powerful, dynamic, life-changing things you will ever do in the Kingdom of God...TNT...they Take No Talent! The Power of God is enough.

Fear attempts to contain us in the corral of can't. Fear attempts to convince us that we aren't enough. It looms over us and goads us until we tell ourselves:

- *"I can't survive this."*
- *"I can't do that."*
- *"I can't succeed."*
- *"I can't learn this."*
- *"I can't do any better."*
- *"I can't measure up."*
- *"I can't see the sunshine."*
- *"I can't see tomorrow."*
- *"I can't make it."*

But no matter what lies fear has fed us and no matter how big the problem may seem, God is greater. God is bigger. God is stronger. God is more powerful. That's why Paul wrote to the Corinthian church and said, *"That your faith should not stand in the wisdom of men, but in the power of God."* (I Corinthians 2:5) The power of God will always overshadow the wisdom of man.

The Psalmist declared: *"The Voice of the Lord is powerful; the voice of the Lord is full of majesty."* (Psalm 29:4) Here's the best part, the Voice of the Lord is speaking to us in this hour and He says, *"Fear not!"*

LOVE
Love is the second weapon God has placed in our arsenal to defeat fear. The Apostle John wrote the following about the relationship between fear and love: *"There is no fear in love; but perfect love casteth out fear: because fear hath torment. He that feareth is not made perfect in love"* (1 John 4:18).

Love and fear are like oil and water. They don't mix. Love casts out fear and there is no fear in love. It's fitting that II Timothy 1:7 and I John 4:18 use the same word for "love." It's no surprise to most that the Greek word here is *agape*. It describes not the love of man, but rather the love of God.

Theologian James Packer once wrote *agape* seems to have been an entirely Christian construct. It isn't found in any Greek literature prior to the writing of the New Testament. The only other major source where *agape* is found is in the *Septuagint*, the Greek Old Testament, and even then, it's still only used to describe God's love.

Packer theorized it was the Early Church that first coined the term. First Century Christians created a new, more excellent word to express this new, more excellent thing they had discovered (I Corinthians 12:31). The existing Greek words for love didn't do God's love justice. Their culture couldn't define it, the arts couldn't express it, and their existing words couldn't describe it. Every tool at their disposal—including a language that even today is known for its ability to describe abstract ideas with pinpoint accuracy—fell miserably short. So, Christians took the next logical step and they made up their own word, *agape,* to describe the perfect, completely selfless, love of God.[4]

It's this love that's described in John 3:16 when it says, *"For God so loved the world, that He gave…"* It's this love that's described in Romans 5:8, where Paul writes, *"But God commendeth His love toward us, in that, while we were yet sinners, Christ died for us."* He continues the thought two verses later in Romans 5:10, writing that when we were still the enemies of God, we were reconciled unto Him by the cross of Calvary.

Later in the Book of Romans, Paul would pen these words describing the endless, boundless love of God: *"For I am persuaded, that neither death, nor life, nor angels, nor principalities, nor powers, nor things present, nor things to come, nor height, nor depth, nor any other creature, shall be able to separate us from the love of God, which is in Christ Jesus our Lord"* (Romans 8:38-39).

---

[4] Packer, James. "Your Father Loves You." Harold Shaw Publishers, 1986, page for March 10.

God loves you. God loves me. God loves us. And if He loves us, what do we have to fear? *"If God be for us, who can be against us?"* (Romans 8:31) We don't have to fear because *"in all these things we are more than conquerors through Him that loved us"* (Romans 8:37). I believe that if we were to ever truly catch a glimpse of the love God has for us, the grip of irrational fear would loosen and fade away. The third verse of one of my favorite hymns, *"Love of God,"* describes it this way:

> *Could we with ink the ocean fill,*
> *And were the skies of parchment made;*
> *Were every stalk on earth a quill,*
> *And every man a scribe by trade;*
> *To write the Love of God above*
> *Would drain the ocean dry;*
> *Nor could the scroll contain the whole,*
> *Though stretched from sky to sky.* [5]

Fear is a pitiful servant and a horrible taskmaster. Allow it to fester in your heart and it will undermine the best laid plans and intentions. Fear brings torment and torment is not of God (I John 4:18). Love casts out all fear, and in the process provides peace that exceeds all understanding (Philippians 4:7).

Hello, love. Goodbye, fear.

A SOUND MIND
The third weapon we have against fear is a sound mind. Paul lists this one last because once we understand God's power and have chosen to rest in His love, sound thinking cannot help but follow. I remember vividly the last service our church held before COVID-19 was declared a pandemic and churches were asked to suspend services. During the song service, we hit the bridge to one of our commonly sung worship songs. It's an anthem, almost a chant or rallying cry. And, suddenly, a wave of fresh faith filled the house. We were encouraged. We were

---

[5] Words & Music © 1923, Ren. 1951 by Hope Publishing Co., Carol Stream, IL 60188.

triumphant. No matter what might come, we were victorious. Even in the face of uncertainty, as one body, our entire congregation lifted their voices together and loudly proclaimed:

Our God is in Control
Steadfast, Unmovable
Nothing's Impossible
Our God Reigns
Forever [6]

That may not seem logical in the face of a global pandemic. But it IS sound thinking considering the God we serve! We can rejoice even in uncertainty because God is in control. He has all power and we are His people. I believe it's this same spirit of worship David exhibited when he wrote:

"Make a joyful noise unto the Lord, all ye lands. Serve the Lord with gladness: come before His Presence with singing. Know ye that the Lord He is God: it is He that hath made us, and not we ourselves; we are His people, and the sheep of His pasture. Enter into His gates with thanksgiving, and into His courts with praise: be thankful unto Him, and bless His Name. For the Lord is good; His mercy is everlasting; and His truth endureth to all generations!" (Psalm 100:1-5)

Our logical conclusion, in light of God's greatness, is to assume He is in full control. And, we can place our trust in Him. The word for "sound mind" in II Timothy 1:7 is *sophroneo*. It's a compound word made up of two other Greek words: *sodzo* and *phroneo*. *Sodzo* carries with it the idea of something that has been saved or delivered and is now safe and secure. Culturally, the meaning goes deeper. It depicts *"a person who was on the verge of death but then was revived and resuscitated because new life was breathed into him."* [7] How awesome is that!

---

[6] Houghton, Israel & Putnam, BJ. "Our God Reigns." RGM New Breed Music, 2015.

[7] Renner, Rick. *Sparkling Gems from the Greek.* 1st ed., Teach All Nations. 2003, p. 73.

The word *phroneo* refers to our intellectual mind, the part of our brain responsible for making decisions. It is our total system of thought, our complete frame of mind. It's the part of us that not only regulates our decisions, but also controls our emotions, actions, and reactions.

The complete picture Paul is painting is of a mind that has been fully transformed by the death, burial and resurrection of Jesus Christ (I Corinthians 15:1-4; Acts 2:38). It is a mind that has died out to its former nature and its former way of thinking. It is a person *"transformed by the renewing of [their] mind."* (Romans 12:2) Paul expressed this same concept in a slightly different manner when he wrote:

"And have put on the new man, which is renewed in knowledge after the image of Him that created him." (Colossians 3:10)

As such, the saved not only have a new lease on life, but a new outlook on it as well. *"Not by works of righteousness which we have done, but according to His mercy He saved us, by the washing of regeneration, and renewing of the Holy Ghost"* (Titus 3:5).

The renewed mind has been *"delivered, rescued, revived, salvaged, and protected and is now safe and secure"* from the *"illogically absurd, ridiculous, unfounded and crazy thoughts"* that had previously taken control. [8]

Having a sound mind is imperative, especially when we consider fear's effect upon it. Fear fuels imbalanced, rash thinking. Science calls this a fight-or-flight response. In moments of danger, key systems in our body kick into overdrive and others (like logical thinking) take a backseat to impulsive, life-preserving action. When we operate out of fear, we're willing to sacrifice everything to survive. We may not feel physical terror toward a person or situation, but if we make a move out of self-preservation, the chances we are driven by fear are very high. Fear is either focused on the here-and-now or on the frightful unknown. Either

---

[8] Ibid. See End Note 7.

way, logic and soundness of mind take a back seat to emotional and adrenaline-driven action.

In the right context, this is a powerful defense mechanism, but living in fear isn't sustainable.

The power of a sound mind makes sense, especially when we see the interplay between fear and our behavior. I referenced this before in my book, _Let's Be Honest: Living a Life of Radical, Biblical Integrity_, but it's worth repeating. If we really think about it, most of the carnal, selfish decisions we make are rooted in fear. Whether it's fearing the loss of popularity, fear-driven self-preservation, putting others down to boost our feelings of self-worth, or avoiding conflict altogether, all of those motivations find their basis in fear.

Is it any wonder salvation is hailed a helmet in the Armor of God? (Isaiah 59:17; Ephesians 6:17) When we realize irrational fear is an attack on our mind, it becomes even more relevant in that regard. Paul takes it a step further in I Thessalonians 5:8, saying it's not just salvation, but the HOPE of salvation that is a helmet to the believer. We have soundness of mind in times of uncertainty because, in God, we have hope!

Standing firm in the promises of God, seeing Him for who He is, we can emphatically, confidently tell fear to take a hike and hit the road. As a believer, you have the freedom to banish fear _"because greater is He that is in you, than he that is in the world."_ (1 John 4:4)

So, lace up your bootstraps and arm yourself. You've been issued the "Big Three" by your Commander-in-Chief, freshly commissioned from the Armory of Heaven: _Power, Love, and a Sound Mind._ It's time to take on fear...and win! Remember, we always triumph in Him! (II Corinthians 2:14)

CHAPTER THREE

The Bank of Hope

"I have set the Lord always before me: because He is at my right hand,
I shall not be moved. Therefore my heart is glad, and my
glory rejoiceth: my flesh also shall rest in hope."
(Psalm 16:8-9)

I first heard of the Bank of Hope on a minister's forum, proposed as a seed thought. [9] It was highlighted for the very reason you might imagine: *The title alone could "preach."*

Formed from a merger on July 29, 2016 and boasting 58 branches, the Bank of Hope in Los Angeles prides itself as *"The Only Super Regional Korean-American Bank in the U.S."* As a financial institution, it serves as a fiscal intersection, a place where two nations meet.

It's the same in the spiritual. Hope is the best kind of intersection. In our case, it is where Heaven meets Earth. Part of the model Jesus used to teach His disciples to pray contained these words: *"Thy Kingdom come, Thy Will be done in Earth, as it is in Heaven."* (Matthew 6:10). It makes sense because the God of Earth is also the God of Heaven, and His Will, will ultimately be done in both (Revelation 11:4; 11:13; 16:11). After all, Heaven is His throne, and Earth is His footstool. (Isaiah 66:1; Acts 7:49)

Hope is where spiritual things become tangible. As such, the idea of hope is very closely related to faith. There's a distinction between the concepts, which is why they're listed separately in I Corinthians 13:13, but, they are also integral to each other. So much so, that hope is

---

[9] Here's looking at you, Scott Phillips, Kevin Shindoll, and the rest of WordShare.

included as part of faith's definition in Hebrews 11:1: *"Now faith is the substance of things hoped for, the evidence of things not seen."*

In our modern culture, we use hope in the sense of *"I hope it works out"* or *"I hope this happens."* Ironically, the secular meaning of hope denotes uncertainty, while the Scriptural definition does the exact opposite. Hope in Scripture is best expressed as anticipation. It's an expectation of good things. In the Biblical sense, hope is not a matter of "if" as much as a matter of "when."

Isn't that encouraging? The Master's version of hope outweighs and out-performs the version of the masses. If that's true of hope's definition, how much truer is it, of hope's function in life!

As believers we can have hope, even in a climate of fear. We hope because we trust. We anticipate God will stand behind His Word. We expect He will come through. We know He is ever true and faithful. We're confident He is in full control.

Hope is an advantage unbelievers will never fully understand. When our hope is in God, we already know the end of the story before it ever unfolds. We triumph in Him! (II Corinthians 2:14) The writer of Hebrews put it this way: *"Let us hold fast the profession of our faith without wavering; for He is faithful that promised."* (Hebrews 10:23). The rendering of this verse in the NIV says, *"Let us hold unswervingly to the hope we profess..."*

In the worst-case scenario, if our life were to become a treacherous, painful wreck of chaos, it's a moot point because, even then, we have the hope of eternity! As he faced certain death, the Apostle Paul didn't look into the future and see impending doom. No! Instead, he said: *"For to me to live is Christ, and to die is gain"* (Philippians 1:21). Paul is proclaiming, *"If I live, I win. If I die, I win all the more."*

Best of all, God isn't just the God Who **has** hope. Scripture says He's the God **of** hope! Read it for yourself! *"Now the God of hope fill you with* *all joy and peace in believing, that ye may abound in hope, through the power of the Holy Ghost."* (Romans 15:13)

The reason we abound in hope isn't because we have a positive mindset or because of something we've done in our own power. The ability to abound in hope comes from the Presence of God, the Holy Spirit, being ever-present in our lives. And the God we serve isn't just the God of Hope, He's also the God of Patience and Consolation (Romans 15:5), the God of All Grace (I Peter 5:10), the God of All Comfort (II Corinthians 1:3), the God of Glory (Acts 7:2), the God of the Living (Matthew 22:32), and the God of Love (II Corinthians 13:11).

THE PEACE OF GOD

Out of all the "God of" titles in the New Testament, care to guess which occurs most often? It's probably the one we need most in times of uncertainty. Again and again, we are told He is the God of Peace (Romans 15:33; 16:20; Philippians 4:9; I Thessalonians 5:23; Hebrews 13:20).

I'm thankful for the peace of God. It is the peace that passes all understanding (Philippians 4:7). The prophet Isaiah penned these words under the inspiration of the Holy Spirit. They're especially fitting and worthy of being remembered in times of uncertainty: *"Thou wilt keep him in perfect peace, whose mind is stayed on Thee: because he trusteth in Thee"* (Isaiah 26:3). The Book of Romans proclaims that God gives us joy and peace, so we can *"abound in hope,"* no matter life's circumstances (Romans 15:33).

HEAVEN'S BANK OF HOPE

Rest assured, Heaven's Bank of Hope will never go bankrupt. In an earthly system, we can only withdraw according to what we've deposited. In the natural, if you deposit $200 into your bank account, you then have $200 to withdraw when you need it. But, as we store up Heavenly things—items like love, joy, and peace—we're investing them in a joint account. We are joint heirs with Him after all (Romans 8:17). We're not the only one making deposits! For every bit of hope we add, God is always depositing more.

I believe that's one aspect of Proverbs 21:21: *"He that followeth after righteousness and mercy findeth life, righteousness, and honour."* No matter what we deposit, there's always abundantly more to withdraw. Those who deposit righteousness and mercy into Heaven's Bank of Hope don't just find those things. They also find life and honor. We can never drain Heaven's Bank of Hope. The well will never run dry (Isaiah 58:11).

HIS MERCY ENDURES FOREVER

If you do a quick search for the phrase *"His mercy endureth for ever"* within the pages of the Bible, you'll find it's fairly common. It occurs 41 times in Scripture, overall. Ezra and Jeremiah both proclaimed it at different times in their ministry (Ezra 3:11; Jeremiah 33:11). David charged a choir to sing it in His Tabernacle (I Chronicles 16:34, 41). It was sung at the dedication of Solomon's Temple (II Chronicles 5:13). And, it was chanted before Jehoshaphat's troops as they went into battle (II Chronicles 20:21).

The most famous occurrence of *"His mercy endureth for ever"* is in Psalm 136. This Psalm stands out from all others in that each of its verses ends with the phrase. We may not know the author and there's debate about its time period, but here's what we do know: **Psalm 136 was written with purpose.** All Scripture is, of course, but this passage is even more so. It serves as a summary, a synopsis, an encapsulation of ancient Israeli culture. It describes the history and identity of Israel in a nutshell. Concerning this portion of Scripture, one famous commentator wrote: *"The Psalm turns history into theology and theology into worship."* [10]

Each line and idea defines Israel in relation to something else, to Someone else. In each verse of the Psalm, Israel is defined by their

---

[10] Wiersbe, Warren. "The Wiersbe Bible OT Commentary." Published by David C. Cook. Colorado Springs, CO. Page 1036. Second Edition, 2007.

relationship with God. As the profile of God comes into focus, the personality of Israel does the same. Here is how He's described:

- **The Creator:** *"The One Who Brings Us Forth"* (v. 1-9)
- **The Redeemer:** *"The One Who Brings Us Out"* (v. 10-12)
- **The Shepherd:** *"The One Who Brings Us Through"* (v. 13-16)
- **The Conqueror:** *"The One Who Brings Us In"* (v. 17-22)
- **The Deliverer:** *"The One Who Brings Us Back"* (v. 23-26) [11]

As God walks Israel through their own timeline, He outlines their identity. He lays out their history, saying *"This is who you are...and it's because of Me."* Coupled with every description of the Creation, every account of overthrown kings, every instance of redemption in the Exodus, this one phrase repeated over and over, serves as an explanation for everything that's done. Transcribed directly into Israel's ancestral and cultural DNA is the understanding that the mercy of the Lord endures forever.

David echoed the idea in Psalm 23 when he wrote: *"He restoreth my soul: He leadeth me in the paths of righteousness for His Name's sake"* (Psalm 23:4). Notice that last phrase, *"for His Name's sake."* Everything God does in our lives is for the furthering of His Glory and of His Name. Every good and perfect thing ties back to the eternal identity of God. And while that is enough, God takes it a step further. Why? Because He's crazy about us.

The term *"mercy"* in Psalm 136 is most literally translated as the word *"lovingkindness."* A more common synonym for lovingkindness is compassion.

Consider all the times the Gospels record Jesus was moved with compassion. His compassion, His mercy, His lovingkindness spurred Him to move. The onus of it all is this: **The God of the Universe...loves**

---

[11] Ibid. See End Note 10.

you. Not because He HAS to, but because He has chosen to. Why would we ever resist the urge to trust Him?

God's compassion, mercy, and lovingkindness has no bounds, which provides us with ultimate hope. In Jeremiah 29:11, God's man of the hour prophesies the following, speaking over God's Chosen People:

"For I know the thoughts that I think toward you, saith the Lord, thoughts of peace, and not of evil, to give you an expected end." (Jeremiah 29:11)

We use this verse when we find ourselves in need of encouragement. It serves as a reminder to the believer that God is in control. But, there's more happening here in this verse. When God makes this proclamation, Israel is not in a good place.

At this point in history, they've rejected Him time and again. They've chased after idols. They've killed the prophets of God. God, in His mercy, would send men with a message from Him and they would chase each one down, torture him, and kill him.

Even Jeremiah, the man who's speaking on God's behalf in this instance, isn't immune to this treatment. He was beaten. Then, they put him in a stockade, burned his scrolls, threw him in a pit, cursed him, and left him to starve and die (Jeremiah 20:1-2; 26:11; 36:23; 38:6; 43:2).

Still, God begins to speak to Jeremiah with compassion and says: *"I want to give my people a promise. I know what they've done. I know what they're doing. I know where their hearts are right now. But My mercy, My love, My lovingkindness, My compassion...is greater."* And it's those people—the very people who have rejected Him and are now in a dire situation of their own making—to whom God speaks.

- They have no inkling of the depth of His love. Still, He says: *"For I know the thoughts that I think toward you."*

- They've made war and fought Him at every turn and, yet, the only thoughts He has toward them are *"thoughts of peace."*

- Though they've done evil, the thoughts He has toward them are *"not of evil."*

- And despite every rebellious action, God still seeks to give them *"an expected end,"* having a greater destiny in mind for them than they could ever comprehend.

Oh, how great! How deep! How wide is the love and mercy of God for His people! God's promise is given in Jeremiah 29:11. The reason why is given exactly 4 chapters later, in Jeremiah 33:11. Resting directly in the center of that verse, we find this familiar phrase: *"for the Lord is good; for His mercy endureth for ever:"*

Why would we ever choose to doubt and fear? He has established the Bank of Hope on our behalf. We have access to every good thing under Heaven. We have the promise of eternity. Best of all, we know the One who is not only the God of Hope—He is hope Himself. Paul put it this way: *"Christ in you, the Hope of Glory."* (Colossians 1:27)

Jesus—the Hope of Glory—is greater than fear! When we learn to rest in His love and compassion toward us, we find hope and no longer have to fear! As David well said: *"I have set the Lord always before me: because He is at my right hand, I shall not be moved. Therefore my heart is glad, and my glory rejoiceth: my flesh also shall rest in hope."* (Psalm 16:8-9)

CHAPTER FOUR

Jesus is Greater Than Fear

"So that we may boldly say, The Lord is my Helper,
and I will not fear what man shall do unto me."
(Hebrews 13:6)

Today, the skyscraper is called 28 Liberty Street. It was formerly known as the Chase Manhattan Bank Building, or One Chase Manhattan Plaza, depending on the presumptuousness of the person giving directions. A 60-story behemoth, construction began on the skyscraper in 1959. When the project was almost halfway through, a discovery of the worst kind was made. The building had been built on quicksand.

No one knows how that fact fell through the cracks, but one thing was sure: it had to be fixed. Of course, the quicksand would harden on its own, in a million years or so, geologists explained. By then it would be too late. The building would've eventually sunk, tilted, and toppled over, destroying downtown Manhattan with it.

Solutions of all kinds were proposed. Some were better than others. Finally, what was regarded as the best one came about. Crews decided to sink pipes straight down into the ground, infiltrating the quicksand barrier. They then forced a chemical concoction of sodium silicate and calcium chloride down the pipes. This in turn, they theorized, would cause a chemical reaction, transforming the quaggy quicksand into sturdy sandstone. It worked! Construction continued and the building still stands to this day. [12]

---

[12] Peale, Norman Vincent, The Amazing Results of Positive Thinking (New York: Simon & Schuster, 1959), 10.

When I first heard this story, I immediately began to think about what Jesus does in our lives. He alone, through the infusion of the Gospel, can turn our instability to stability, turn pain to purpose, and fear to faith. He is able to take the shaky instances of our lives and mold and make them into a sturdy foundation worthy of construction. It reminds me of the words of David:

"He brought me up also out of an horrible pit, out of the miry clay, and set my feet upon a rock, and established my goings." (Psalm 40:2)

We don't serve the God Who plays according to our rules or Who is bound by the things that bind us. Our God is not restricted by our restrictions. We serve the God who takes soil in one Hand and spit in the other, and mashes them together to make something new (Genesis 2:7; John 9:6).

We can place our trust in Him. If we can trust Him with the hereafter, how is it that we struggle to trust Him in the here-and-now? Louie Giglio famously said, *"Fear is faith in the enemy."* [13] If I truly believe God is greater, I can put my trust in Him. I don't want my faith in anything else to be greater than my faith in God, especially not in the enemy of my soul.

I'm in a much better place spiritually, mentally, and emotionally when I am more focused on the person of Jesus than the problem of Jeremy. Listen to the words of the Apostle Peter: *"Casting all your care upon Him; for He careth for you."* (I Peter 5:7)

There's a pivotal play on words here. The first care is our care which by its very nature, is imperfect and flawed. Those cares are our anxieties. Anxiety is a critical point in the fear-faith spectrum. It's the tipping point where we go from controlling fear to allowing fear to control us. The fact we have fear, doesn't mean fear has to have us.

---

[13] Giglio, Louie. "Fear is faith in the enemy." www.facebook.com/officialLouieGiglio/posts/fear-is-faith-in-the-enemy/929501203892590. February 24, 2018. Accessed May 2, 2020.

Arthur Somers Roche once said, *"Anxiety is a thin stream of fear trickling through the mind. If encouraged, it cuts a channel into which all others thoughts are drained."* [14] You've heard the phrase actions speak louder than words, right? This is a perfect example. Our thoughts control our actions and our actions emphatically declare where our faith is placed. Does that mean we are reckless or irresponsible? Not at all. We all have actions to take and duties to perform, but what changes is our internal perception of how those duties are carried out. Because now, we're not entangled in a spider's web of what-ifs. We respect our responsibilities instead of fearing them. Remember, fear is based on feelings, while respect is based on the real.

We take anxiety—this imperfect, flawed human version of "care"—and we cast it upon Jesus. He responds in kind with true, perfect, flawless care. It's a different Greek word entirely. He replaces earthly care with heavenly care. He takes our flawed version, replacing it with what care should be.

We give Him our worry, because, number one, He's asked us to do it. Secondly, we give it to Him because He's big enough and strong enough to carry it. When dealing with circumstances outside of our control, giving our anxiety, angst, and worry to God is a form of faith. We give it to Him, faith-believing He's able to handle it. We declare with our actions that Jesus is greater than our fear. Sinclair B. Ferguson said it well when he wrote: *"The fear of the Lord tends to take away all other fears...This is the secret of Christian courage and boldness."* [15]

THE GOD OF [INSERT YOUR NAME HERE]

Last chapter, we discussed the *"God of"* statements, mostly focusing on the New Testament. There's a fascinating phenomenon that occurs when we consider both the Old and New Testaments. There are a myriad of mentions of God as the *"God of Abraham,"* or the *"God of Isaac,"* or

---

[14] Roche, Arthur Somers. "Thoughts on the Business of Life." Forbes Magazine. https://www.forbes.com/quotes/789/. Accessed May 3, 2020.

[15] Ferguson, Sinclair B., Grow in Grace by permission of Banner of Truth (Carlisle, PA: Banner of Truth, 1989), 33-34.

the *"God of David"* in the Old Testament. The number of those types of mentions outweighs almost all other references to God.

As awesome as it is that He is the God of hope, patience, grace, comfort, glory, love, and peace, it means the most that He is the God of Jeremy. ***He is the God of [insert your name here].*** He is not just God, out there, somewhere. He is my God. He is your God. And if He hasn't become that yet in your life, He can be, if you'll only allow Him! Jesus is not content to sit on the fringes of your life. He desires to be with us. He asks us to take every aspect of our life, every element of the unknown, and to cast it all upon Him.

Because He cares not just for us…but for you, personally.

WORSHIP VS. PRAISE

We've all heard the terms "worship" and "praise." Most tend to use them interchangeably and they are powerful when used in combination. While there are some similarities, there is a primary difference as well. The single element that separates worship from praise is level of intimacy. Praise, as powerful as it is, is generic. Worship is intimate. Worship requires at least some form of relationship. Praise loudly proclaims, *"He is God, Savior, and King!"* Worship emphatically whispers, *"He is MY God, MY Savior, and MY King."* While the words of praise may be true, worship's perspective is infinitely more powerful. A life-altering transformation occurs when we allow God to become *"our God."*

No one, no matter their standing with God, is immune from distress. Read through the Psalms and you'll quickly find even David, the man after God's own heart, had his share. A familiar example of this is I Samuel 30:

"And David was greatly distressed; for the people spake of stoning him, because the soul of all the people was grieved, every man for his sons and for his daughters: but David encouraged himself in the Lord his God." (I Samuel 30:6)

Talk about a bad day! David's kingdom was raided and several of his people were captured, including members of his own family. It's also a political nightmare. His popularity is at its absolute lowest. So low, in fact, the Kingdom is calling for his head! He has no one. His friends are gone, hope seems to be lost, and, as fear, worry, doubt and discouragement begin to creep into his mind, the king takes action. We see what he does at the end of that verse: *"but David encouraged himself in the Lord his God."*

David didn't encourage himself in his call, his crown, or his accomplishments. He didn't encourage himself in his stuff or his money. He definitely didn't encourage himself in his friends because they were all long gone.

No matter how faithful our friends and family may be, no one can be with us 24 / 7 / 365, patting our back and telling us it's going to be alright. There will ultimately be times when it is just us and our problem and those can either be moments of anxiety or encouragement. The deciding factor is what we choose to do.

David chose to encourage himself, but **how** he did it is what's most important. David didn't just encourage himself in God Almighty. He encouraged himself in the Lord HIS God.

That's relationship.

That's connection.

That's personal.

David looked away from his problem and began to look at his God. I imagine David probably said something along the lines of, *"God, I know You're the God of Israel, but I need You to be the God of David right now."* When David looked to Providence instead of his problem, God provided a solution and gave him a victorious plan of attack. How encouraging!

In a time of unparalleled uncertainty, David tethers himself to his relationship with God. We should be willing to do the same, knowing God is greater than our fear, greater than our distress, greater than our discouragement, greater than our angst, and greater than our anxiety. In addition to being greater than every situation and problem, God is also greater than our heart, the things within it, and any troubles we could dream up or imagine. The Apostle John put it this way: *"And hereby we know that we are of the truth, and shall assure our hearts before him. For if our heart condemn us, God is greater than our heart, and knoweth all things."* (1 John 3:19-20)

CAMP OUT IN THE PSALMS

A good piece of advice, if you find yourself discouraged, is to camp out in the Psalms and allow faith to feed your soul (Romans 10:17). In that book alone, there are 75 verses mentioning the word fear, 55 verses with mentions of trouble, 14 of the word afraid, 9 of distress, and 5 uses of the word terror. Yet, the prevailing theme is God is in control. Which is why we can say what the Psalmist said: *"What time I am afraid, I will trust in Thee."* (Psalm 56:3)

It's also why he wrote the following in confidence: *"The Lord also will be a Refuge for the oppressed, a Refuge in times of trouble."* (Psalm 9:9).

It's why he famously proclaimed: *"Yea, though I walk through the valley of the shadow of death, I will fear no evil: for Thou art with me; Thy rod and Thy staff they comfort me."* (Psalm 23:4) You are not alone. Fear does not have to be your default setting. Jesus, the Good Shepherd, is with you and He is greater than fear.

Hard times will come. Our promise is that God will be with us in those times of danger and uncertainty. The writer of Hebrews calls back to the Psalms when he writes: *"So that we may boldly say, The Lord is my Helper, and I will not fear what man shall do unto me"* (Hebrews 13:6;

See Psalm 118:6,7). We can walk with confidence, knowing God is with us, no matter the circumstances.

UNDER THE SUN

The opening chapter of Ecclesiastes has some eye-opening things to say concerning the state of our world. Solomon is the author of Ecclesiastes. He's also the writer for most of the Book of Proverbs. Though both books are written by the same man, they are also written from completely different perspectives. There's an internal tension pulling between the books; two vantage points grappling for control.

Proverbs is written at the beginning of Solomon's life when he is most pursuant of God. It's a portrait of the Wisdom of God. There's an undeniable, underlying sense of hope scattered throughout its pages. Through every verse, there's an unspoken assurance that God is in control. Peace is contained in the pages of Proverbs.

Later in Solomon's life, something changes. He forms treaties with foreign nations and marries into alliances of idolatry. He places his trust in chariots and technology. Over time, Solomon begins to serve other gods. He transitions from allowing idol worship to occur in his house to becoming an active participant.

To use modern church terminology, you could say Solomon backslides. It's here in this fallen state and backslidden existence he writes the Book of Ecclesiastes. While Proverbs is the wisdom of God, this new book becomes the opposite. It's an ode to the wisdom of man without God. Gone is the underlying sense of hope contained in his former writings. Instead, he laments over and over again—33 times in fact—life is hopeless. Solomon writes: *"Vanity of vanities...all is vanity."* (Ecclesiastes 12:8). The premise of the entire book is life ultimately has no meaning and is pointless. Such is the perspective of man without God.

In the opening chapter, however, Solomon creates a list of givens. He mentions generations will rise and fall (v. 4) and the sun will do the same

(v. 5). He describes the winds and their circuits (v. 6) and the character of the seas (v. 7). On and on he goes, listing out the things that can never change. He summarizes it all in the beginning of verse 9, when he says: *"The thing that hath been, it is that which shall be; and that which is done is that which shall be done: and there is no new thing…"* (v. 9a)

It is what it is; it will be what it will be. But then, Solomon adds another curious phrase. One that only shows up in Ecclesiastes, but appears 27 times throughout the book. Solomon makes his statement and then adds three little words: *Under. The. Sun.*

"There is no new thing under the sun" (Ecclesiastes 1:9b)

The phrase "under the sun" is a Jewish idiom. It's a cultural statement with a deeper meaning. We use idioms all the time. When we say, *"a bird in the hand is worth two in the bush,"* we're not talking about literal birds and bushes. We're talking about being appreciative of what we have. It's an idiom, a cultural statement with a deeper meaning. The phrase *"under the sun"* works the same way.

In laymen's terms, *"under the sun"* means *"everything outside of God."* When we say there's nothing new under the sun, we're saying there's nothing new…outside of God. Even in his hopelessness, when it comes to newness and when it comes to life, empty, hollow Solomon still has the semblance of mind to say: *"There's nothing new in life…EXCEPT when God's involved."* Even the wisdom of man cannot argue with God's greatness. The deepest depths of disparity have no answer for His Majesty!

The Savior we serve does not operate solely under the sun. We serve the God Who's above it! He's beyond the influence of the sun. He's beyond the boundaries of the natural. We serve the God above every system, every situation and every circumstance. Our God does not serve the sun; He created it!

And, the Creator is always greater than the creation.

When describing Jesus in the introduction to his gospel account, John wrote: *"In the beginning was the Word, and the Word was with God, and the Word was God. The same was in the beginning with God. All things were made by Him; and without Him was not any thing made that was made."* (John 1:1-3) He builds upon this idea in verse 10 of the same chapter, adding: *"He was in the world, and the world was made by Him, and the world knew Him not."* (John 1:10)

Paul echoed this same idea in 1 Corinthians 8:6, when he wrote: *"Yet for us there is but one God, the Father, from Whom all things came and for Whom we exist. And there is but one Lord, Jesus Christ, through Whom all things came and through Whom we exist."* He declared the same truth about Jesus in a slightly different way in the Book of Colossians: *"For in Him dwelleth all the fulness of the Godhead bodily."* (Colossians 2:9)

And if that weren't enough, Jesus Himself, declares *"'I am Alpha and Omega, the Beginning and the Ending,' saith the Lord, 'Which is, and Which was, and Which is to come, the Almighty.'"* (Revelation 1:8) In fact, the entire purpose of the Book of Revelation—where this quote comes from—is given in its first verse. Namely, to serve as the *"Revelation of Jesus Christ"* (Revelation 1:1). The closing book of the Bible has a purpose beyond prophecy, symbol, and visions. It's more than a series of symbols and visions. It's a declaration that no matter what happens, whatever comes our way, Jesus is King! He alone is in control. He rules and He reigns! We do not have to fear!

Jesus is greater than fear.

Jesus is greater than the world and everything that exists within it. As we explore the entire counsel of Scripture, we see for every process Solomon mentions and every assumption he makes in the first few verses of Ecclesiastes, God provides a supernatural response. God's wisdom both outweighs and outperforms the wisdom of man:

47

- Man says things are set (v. 2), but God says, *"Behold, I will do a new thing!"* (Isaiah 43:19)

- Man says things are what they are (v. 4), but God says: *"Behold, I make all things new!"* (Rev. 21:5)

- Man says, *"The earth abideth for ever"* (v. 4), but we serve the God Who spoke the worlds into existence (Psalm 33:9) and He is also the One Who said: *"Heaven and Earth shall pass away, but My words shall not pass away."* (Matt. 24:35)

- Man says, *"The sun also ariseth, and the sun goeth down."* (v. 5). But we serve the God Who says: *"Sun, stand still!"* and the sun stops for Joshua (Joshua 10:12-13). We serve the God Who says: *"Sun, go backward! Prove My promises are sure to Hezekiah!"* and the sun obeys. (Isaiah 38:4-9)

- Man says the wind blows according to its circuits (v. 6). It can't be controlled. But we serve the God David said walks *"on the wings of the wind"* (Psalm 104:3). We serve the God Who rebukes the wind, saying: *"Peace be still!"* and storms stop! (Mark 4:39)

- Man says the seas can't be controlled (v. 7). But we serve the God Who walks on water. Job said God treads on the waves (Job 9:8). David said He sits *"upon the flood"* (Ps. 29:10). Mark wrote the waves obey Him (Mk. 4:41) and Psalm 93:3 says the floods lift up their voices and even their waves in praise!

No matter what man says, God is greater. The actions above are impossible and, yet, still performed and documented by our God. He is not only able, but also willing to act! He has an answer for every question, a solution for every problem. For every fear, He offers faith, hope, and love. We can place our trust in Him!

LIFT UP MY EYES

Several of my favorite verses of Scripture come from the book of Psalms, but one particularly stands out in light of everything we face: *"I will lift up mine eyes unto the hills, from whence cometh my help. My help cometh from the Lord, Which made Heaven and Earth"* (Psalm 121:1-2). The Hebrew word for "keep" is repeated 6 times in Psalm 121, emphasizing again and again God will not leave, no matter the circumstances. Though commentators disagree on the specifics, they all agree David is describing looking above a pressing problem, catching the peaks of the hills with his eyes, and then choosing to raise his gaze even higher, looking toward Heaven and thanking God for His provision. Like the old hymn so beautifully says:

> *Turn your eyes upon Jesus*
> *Look full in His wonderful face*
> *And the things of earth*
> *Will grow strangely dim*
> *In the light of His glory and grace* [16]

When we lift our eyes and choose to look above our current situation, our mindset changes. In Psalm 16, David is facing a situation with an unknown outcome. Even then, the overarching attitude of the Psalm is positive. In verse 8, he gives the reason, saying, *"I have set the Lord always before me."* And in verse 9, he describes how that decision affects his outlook, saying, *"therefore my heart is glad."* Knowing God is in control levels his emotional stability, even in the face of the unknown. What a promise, especially in our day and age!

God is bigger than our weakness, our enemies, and our needs. He is far more trustworthy than the lies fear has fed us. Satan is the father of lies and Fear is his favored son (John 8:44). Fear plays solely according to the playbook of Hell, seeking to torment, steal, kill, and destroy (John 10:10; I John 4:18). At its core, fear is a liar—the robber of rest—seeking to plant the seed of doubt in our mind, saying:

---

[16] Lemmel, Helen Howarth. "Turn Your Eyes Upon Jesus." Public Domain. 1922.

- *"There is no hope."*
- *"You're headed toward disaster."*
- *"Think of all of the things that could go wrong."*
- *"Your life is a lie."*
- *"People are going to discover how weak you are."*
- *"You're on your own."*
- *"You'll never win."*
- *"It happened to them; you're next!"*

Tell fear to take a hike! I've said it several times throughout the course of this book: **Jesus is greater than your fear.** Don't give in to the deception of doubt. Cling to faith. Use the tools God has given you to defeat fear, especially the "big three" of love, power, and a sound mind. Remind yourself, you are an heir of the Kingdom and Heaven's Bank of Hope will never go bankrupt. Hard times will most assuredly come. Trouble will always rear its ugly head. But, even when the valleys we walk seem like deathtraps, no matter what happens, you are walking with the Good Shepherd. You don't have to fear any evil, because He is with you (Psalm 23:4). Fear is the robber of rest, while Jesus is the Giver of rest and reassurance. He compassionately calls:

"Come unto Me, all ye that labour and are heavy laden, and I will give you rest. Take My yoke upon you, and learn of Me; for I am meek and lowly in heart: and ye shall find rest unto your souls. For My yoke is easy, and My burden is light." (Matthew 11:28-30)

Fear not. Find your rest.

God is here with you, right now. And, He is greater.

AUTHOR'S NOTE:
Thank you for taking the time to read this book. If _Greater Than Fear_ has been a blessing to you, be sure to leave a positive review on Amazon and GoodReads. You can also share it with your friends and colleagues on social media using the hashtag:

#GreaterThanFearBook

Acknowledgements

First and foremost, I want to give honor to the Friend greater than fear. Jesus, my Lord and my King, everything I do is for you. Saturate each word I've written with your anointing, bring hope to the bound, and freedom to the captive.

To Sarah, the love of my life. My favorite editor. Thank you for joining me in this adventure called life (and, now, parenthood). You patiently, yet a little too happily make my manuscripts bleed red ink, but the end-result is always better. So, is the joyful remainder of my life with you...minus the bleeding, of course.

To my parents, especially my Mom, thank you for teaching me to be brave and to always trust the provision of God.

To Truth Youth, the most fearless group of kids I've ever known. You're not kids, of course. You're well on your way to adulthood. But no matter how old you get and how far you go, the Gove's will always call you "our kids." We can't help it. We love you too much to call you anything else.

Pastor and Sis. Jury and our Truth Tabernacle Church Family, thank you for your constant love and support. Thank you for entrusting us with the lives of your students and for being a consistent, genuine example of the Body of Christ. We love you!

To my fellow laborers within the Georgia District, Georgia District Youth Ministries, and Section One Youth, thank you for serving with a Kingdom mindset and a clear standard of excellence. I am honored to be counted among you. I never thought I'd ever be the "old guy" on the Youth Committee, but here we are. Thank you for the continued opportunity to serve.

About the Author

Jeremy Gove is an ordained minister with the United Pentecostal Church International. He is the Student Pastor at Truth Tabernacle in Blackshear, Georgia, under Pastor C.H. Jury. He also serves as the Section One Youth Director for the Georgia District of the UPCI.

Jeremy holds a B.S. in Management Information Systems from the University of Delaware, with a minor in Jewish Studies. He ultimately became one of the first business students at Delaware to hold a minor in that field of study. He currently resides in Blackshear, Georgia with his wife Sarah, their dog, Cuper, and a baby girl on the way.

As the owner of FoxFire Media, Jeremy works as a web designer, marketing consultant, and graphic designer. With a background in both the public and private sectors, he possesses a diverse portfolio of work experience, which includes time spent at 3 of the world's largest Fortune 500 companies. Jeremy is a gifted speaker who teaches with passion and with the goal of applying the Bible's truths and concepts to everyday life. When not teaching, studying, designing, or doing "church work," you can usually find Jeremy sitting down with a good book or spending time with his family.

About the Cover

The cover art for _Greater Than Fear_ carries a very specific message. The black, hatched background represents the darkness of night; the black paint splotches represent the chaos fear brings.

It's a bleak beginning, but, thankfully, the narrative doesn't end there.

There are two other prominent colors on the cover. The white letters reflect the pure light of hope and faith; a light that pierces the darkness and easily overtakes fear when allowed to shine.

The red streaks—particularly the "greater than" symbol—represent the Blood of Jesus Christ. It's a call-back to the Passover, the painting of the doorposts with the blood of a lamb in obedience to the Word of God. It's understood that in a Biblical mindset, doorposts represent the very structural systems of our homes and lives.

In that sense, the Blood of Jesus has been applied to the doorpost of our hearts and gives us victory over doubt and death.

When COVID-19 first broke out, I had several friends place red ribbons on their doors, doorposts, and mailboxes. It was done to serve as a silent witness, a resolved stance declaring God is greater than any sickness or fear. The cover of this book seeks to echo that same sentiment.

Jesus is greater than fear. He is greater than uncertainty. He is greater than doubt and disease. Knowing this, we can confidently stand and rest in His Love.

Made in the USA
Columbia, SC
18 August 2022

65578199R00033